Failed Revolutions

[redacted]